ANCIENT CIVILIZATIONS

Incas

By Duncan Scheff

Raintree Steck-Vaughn Publishers
A Harcourt Company

Austin · New York
www.steck-vaughn.com

Published by Raintree Steck-Vaughn Publishers, an imprint of Steck-Vaughn Company.

Library of Congress Cataloging-in-Publication Data
    Incas/by Duncan Scheff.
        p.cm.—(Ancient civilizations)
    Includes bibliographical references and index.
    ISBN 0-7398-3582-3
    1. Incas—History—Juvenile literature. 2. Incas—Social life and customs—Juvenile literature. [1. Incas. 2. Indians of South America.] I. Title. II. Series.
F3429 .S325 2001
980'.012—dc21

2001019507

Printed and bound in the United States of America
1 2 3 4 5 6 7 8 9 10 WZ 05 04 03 02 01

Produced by Compass Books

Photo Acknowledgments
Archive Photos, 25
Corbis/Kea Publishing Services Ltd., 10; Charles & Josette Lenars, 20, 34;
    Bettmann, 39
Photo Network/Janet Bennet, title page; Carol Christensen, 19, 43;
    William Mitchell, 29, 33; Howard Folsom, 40
Root Resources/Shirley Hodge, 16, 26; Mary and Lloyd McCarthy, 22
Visuals Unlimited/Sylvan H. Witwer, 12, 30; Kjel B. Sandved, 14;
    David Matherly, 36

Content Consultants
Dr. John Hoopes
Department of Anthropology
University of Kansas
Don L. Curry
Educational Author, Editor, Consultant, and Columnist

Contents

Inca History

The Incas had the largest and richest **empire** in the Americas. The empire was made up of many different peoples. They were all under Inca power and united with common laws. These people were all South American Indians, but they spoke different languages and had different **customs**. The Incas were Quechua Indians and spoke the Quechua language. At its height in the 16th century, the Incas ruled more than 14 million people.

The Inca Empire included more than 3,000 miles (4,800 km) of South America. The Incas divided their empire into four parts and called it the land of the four quarters. Their capital city and center of government was Cuzco.

INCA TIMELINE

AD 1200	The first Inca emperor, Manco Capac, begins his rule.
A.D. 1438	The Incas are attacked by the neighboring Chanca people. The emperor's son, Yupanqui, leads the defense and saves Cuzco.
A.D. 1500	European explorers hear stories about Inca wealth and begin searching for the empire.
A.D. 1527	Emperor Huayna Capac dies suddenly of an unknown disease; two of his sons fight for the title of emperor; Atahualpa eventually becomes emperor.
A.D. 1532	Spanish explorer Francisco Pizarro captures and kills Atahualpa.
A.D. 1535	Cuzco falls under Spanish control; the Inca Empire falls.

Beginnings

The Incas had no written language, so the beginnings of the empire are not fully known. Inca stories tell about their **ancestor** named Manco Capac. Some scholars believe he became the Incas' first leader around

A.D. 1200. The Incas believed he was the son of the Sun. Over the next 200 years, the Incas had several more rulers. They became more powerful and built the city of Cuzco.

The Inca Empire began to grow during the early 1400s. Their ruler during this time was called Pachacuti. Pachacuti means "the one who changes the earth" in the Quechua language. He invited neighboring groups of people to join the Inca Empire. He also made the Inca army larger and fought wars to take over land from groups who did not want to join.

The rulers after Pachacuti kept the Inca army strong. They built roads throughout the empire to help the army and other Inca **subjects** travel. Inca rulers fought wars and added more land to the empire. The new people brought into the empire did work for the Inca government. To run the new areas they **captured**, the Incas built new cities and sent governors to these places.

Government

The Incas' government was highly **organized**. There were many laws and rules. Each government **official** had a job to do to make the empire run smoothly. Only people with royal Inca blood or leaders from groups friendly to the Incas could have high government jobs.

The leader of the empire was the emperor, or king, called the Sapa Inca. He was thought to be the son of the Sun. Throughout his life, he was worshiped as a god. He was in charge of religion and the army. The Incas believed all the riches and land in the empire belonged to the emperor.

Each one of the four quarters of the Inca Empire was ruled by a government official called an Apu. The Apus lived in Cuzco and reported to the Sapa Inca.

Local governors lived in the four quarters and made sure that the people were obeying the rules and working for the Incas. These local governors reported to the Apus.

Words to Say

Atahualpa (ot-ah-WAL-pa)
ayllus (EYE-yoos)
Huascar (wass-KAR)
Inti (EEN-tee)
llatu (YA-too)
Manco (MAN-koh)
mit'a (MEET-ah)
orejones (o ray HO-nays)
pukaras (poo-KA-ras)
quena (KAY-na)
quipu (KEE-poo)
quipu camayocs (KEE-poo ka-MY-oks)
Sacsahuaman (sak-sah-wah-MON)

Local leaders who were not of Inca blood helped the Apus run the cities and towns. They were in charge of units of 100, 1,000, and 10,000 families. They divided farming land among these groups. The officials performed marriages and made sure that everyone had food to eat and a place to live.

 This is an ancient Inca storehouse where extra food was kept.

Taxes

There was no money in the Inca Empire. People paid taxes, called mit'a, by working or making things for the government. Farmers worked on lands owned by the government to grow crops for the Sapa Inca. Special craftspeople called camayocs made goods, such as cloth or pots, for the government. These things were stored in giant buildings. If the empire went through hard times, the Sapa Inca would take food or goods out of storage to feed and clothe the people.

Healthy men had to spend time working for the government. They had to serve in the army, build roads and buildings, farm the government's land, or dig for gold and silver.

The Incas had a traveling group of healers called Collahuayas. The Incas treated sickness with magic and with herbs. The Incas sometimes performed surgery on sick or injured people. Scientists have found skulls with healed holes. These show that Inca healers sometimes performed surgery to relieve pressure on the brain caused by blows to the head received during warfare.

This thick stone wall protected an Inca fortress.

Incas and the World

Early in their history, the Incas were at war with many other groups around them. They built their cities on hills or mountains so that they would be hard to attack. They also built special **fortresses**, or strong protected towns. The fortresses were surrounded by tall walls called pukaras. They had towers so soldiers could watch for enemies. The people would move into the fortresses when the Incas were at war with others.

The Incas also became allies with groups that lived around them. An **ally** is a person or country that has a special agreement to support another. With the help of their allies, the Incas were able to control more labor and land.

As their empire grew, the Incas had their subjects build one of the longest road systems in the world at the time. More than 14,000 miles (22,500 km) of roads stretched across the empire. Incas also had people build rope bridges to cross rivers. They built flat steps and roads on steep mountainsides. They used the roads to transport goods across the empire and to trade with other groups in the Andes Mountains and the Pacific coast. Some Inca roads are still used today.

This clay figurine shows what a working-class Inca looked like.

Daily Life of the Incas

People were born into a **social** class based on their family and how rich they were. The Sapa Inca and members of his family were royalty and the most powerful in the Inca world. They lived in large homes, had riches and land, and wore fancy clothes and jewelry.

Nobles were members of ruling Inca families. They had power, land, and riches. They were often priests or held leading jobs in the army or the government.

The working class did most of the work for the government. Most were farmers or shepherds. Shepherds raised and took care of animals, such as llamas and alpacas.

Clothing

Most Incas wore the same general style of
clothing. Women wore a long, sleeveless
dress with a long piece of cloth, called a
mantle, around their shoulders. The dress was
usually tied at the waist with a belt.

Men wore tunics, which are long, straight,
and loose-fitting. Tunics could have short

sleeves or no sleeves and be different lengths. Most men wore short tunics with a loincloth underneath. These long strips of cloth wrapped around the waist, pulled through the legs, and tied in front. Men also wore a sleeveless cloak tied over their shoulders.

The cloth of an Inca's clothing depended on a person's class, job, and **ethnic** group. The cloth was often very colorful and full of lines, triangles, squares, and other geometric shapes. Sometimes craftspeople wove feathers or gold and silver threads into the cloth.

Most clothing was made from the wool of an animal called the alpaca or the llama. Some working-class Incas that lived near the coast of the Pacific Ocean wore cotton clothing.

Nobles wore gold and silver jewelry. Men wore large, heavy gold earrings that stretched their earlobes. Because of this, Spanish people called noble men orejones, or "big ears." Nobles in the government wore a colored headband called a llatu.

Homes

The kind of house a person lived in depended on his or her class, ethnic group, and homeland. Most working-class homes were small and built from bricks of dried mud called adobe. Some people built small, rectangular homes made of stone. They placed grass over wood to make the roofs. The floors were usually dirt.

The homes of the working class generally had only one room and no furniture. People stored items in clay pots and baskets that hung on the walls and roof beams. Family members cooked food on a fire in the center of the room. They ate and slept on mats on the floor.

Often a group of families lived near each other and helped one another farm the land. This group was called an ayllu. Members of an ayllu built houses that faced each other across an open courtyard. The people worked and visited with others in the courtyard.

These stone remains of Inca houses are still standing today.

Inca nobles had larger houses that sometimes had two levels. Their houses were made of stone, and they often decorated the walls with fine cloth as well as silver and gold objects. But, like working-class homes, these homes also had little furniture.

▲ The Incas raised alpacas like this one for meat and for wool to make cloth.

Food

Farming was important to the Inca's way of life. The kinds of crops farmers raised depended on where they lived in the empire. The people who lived by the **tropical** forest grew fruits and peppers. In warm areas they grew squash, beans, and many kinds of corn. They grew potatoes in mountain areas where it was too cold to grow corn.

Potatoes and maize were the most important foods in the Incas diet. The Incas grew about 200 different kinds of potatoes. They learned a special way of saving potatoes so that they would stay fresh for up to five years. They froze the potatoes at night. Then, they dried the potatoes in the sun the next day. Next, the women squeezed the rest of the moisture from the potato and stored it in a clay pot. They put the dried potato flour in water when they were ready to cook it.

Incas who lived near the ocean caught fish and other sea creatures to eat. In the mountains, they hunted rabbits, deer, and wild birds. Some Incas raised guinea pigs for meat. Sometimes people ate llamas and alpaca meat.

The Incas ate stews and soups most of the time. They used chili peppers to flavor many of these dishes.

Today's Incas have kept much of their ancient culture, for example, they still make traditional Inca clothing.

Inca Culture

A group's ideas, customs, traditions, and way of life make up their **culture**. The Incas passed their culture from **generation** to generation through stories, poems, and songs. A generation is a group of people born at about the same time.

Music was especially important to Inca culture. Men and women gathered to sing and dance. Some sang songs telling of Inca history, while others played drums or wind instruments. A wind instrument is a musical instrument played by blowing air into it. One example is the quena, a flute-like recorder made from a reed.

Religion

Religion was an important part of Inca culture. Inca people believed in many gods and goddesses. Their highest god was Inti, the Sun god. The Incas made all of the people in their empire worship and honor the Sun in ceremonies and festivals.

The Incas believed the gods played an important role in their daily lives. Gods of the earth and sky helped the Incas with their crops and with other daily jobs. One of the most important gods was Apu Illapu, the rain god. Farmers asked Apu Illapu to give them rain during dry times.

The Incas held celebrations to honor their gods. One celebration took place before each growing season. The Inca people ate, drank, and danced at this celebration. They hoped this would lead to a good crop.

The Incas also gave offerings to the gods. The Incas believed they could please the gods by giving them gifts. Then, the Incas believed the gods would do good things for them.

▲ This is an Inca temple built to honor the Sun god, Inti.

The Incas built special buildings called temples for their gods. Each Inca city had a special temple for Inti. Priests and the Incas served their gods in the temples. The Incas also made statues of their gods.

▲ **This gold mask was used in religious ceremonies.**

Art

Art was an important part of Inca culture. Highly skilled artists and craftspeople worked full-time making cloth, jewelry, or other items for the nobles.

Some craftspeople made **pottery** out of clay. All of the Inca's beautiful pottery was made by hand coiling rather than on a pottery wheel. Some pottery was for household use, such as pots for cooking. Other pottery was for religious use. Artists painted this pottery with colorful pictures of plants, animals, and gods or goddesses.

Most Inca girls and women learned how to make cloth. They dyed yarn different colors and wove it together to make different colored patterns in the cloth. The patterns showed others who the Incas were, what they did, and where they came from.

The Incas made many items out of metals, such as gold, silver, and copper. They melted the metals and poured them into molds to make small objects, such as axes. They also carefully hammered soft metal into thin sheets that were folded and shaped. They used their skills to create jewelry and ornaments. The Incas often used special stones, such as turquoise, in their jewelry. Another form of Inca artwork was mask making. The Incas created detailed masks for dancing and religious celebrations.

Architecture

The Incas were skilled **architects**. An architect is someone who plans how to make buildings. Before they began building, Inca architects sometimes made models to plan houses and cities. They then explained to stoneworkers what to do to make the building.

Workmen cut giant stones and dragged them to the building site. The Incas traveled by foot and pulled the stones by hand. They used rollers underneath the stones to help move them up and down steep mountains.

Once at the site, workers used tools called chisels and mallets to shape stone blocks. They rubbed wet sand on the blocks to polish the stone. To polish is to rub something to make it smooth. Then they fit the stones together to make walls. Heavy stones were at the bottom. Workers dragged smaller stones up dirt ramps to form the tops of walls.

Inca stoneworkers were highly trained. Their stone blocks were cut so they would fit

▲ Inca builders cut and polished stones so they
would fit together exactly.

together well. They shaped and placed stones
so close together that the blade of a knife
would not fit between them.

The Incas also built stone walls around
some of their cities. These walls protected the
cities from enemy armies. These strong stone
walls still stand at some Inca sites.

▲ These are ancient buildings in the Inca city
of Cuzco.

Cuzco

Cuzco was the center of the Inca Empire.
It is located in a mountain chain known as
the Andes. Cuzco is more than 11,000 feet
(3,800 m) above sea level. Sea level is the
average level of the surface of the ocean.
Cuzco may have had more than 4,000

buildings and may have been home to 200,000 or more people.

Cuzco was planned to look like a giant puma, a kind of mountain lion. It was built in four sections. The sections stood for the four quarters of the empire. Several temples and palaces stood near the center of the city. Many of these buildings were decorated with gold and silver. Rich Inca nobles lived near the center of the city. The working class lived farther out at the edges of the city.

Incas built Cuzco near two rivers so that they could build canals from them. A canal is a human-made waterway. The canals stretched across the length of the city.

Inca soldiers watched Cuzco from a fortress and temple called Sacsahuamon. Its buildings overlook Cuzco from a high hill above the city. Soldiers there warned of enemy attacks.

Cuzco still stands today. More than 250,000 people live there. Thousands of tourists visit Cuzco every year. They come to see the Inca walls and the mountain scenery.

Language and Quipus

The Incas spoke Quechua. This language did not have a written form. Instead of writing things down, the Incas kept track of their history through stories.

The Incas used a system of strings and knots to count. The system was called a **quipu**. A quipu had one main string with many smaller strings of different colors, thicknesses, and types tied to it. Knots on the strings stood for numbers and objects. Government officials used quipus to keep track of taxes, goods, riches, the army, and roads. Incas called quipucamayocs were trained to use the quipu.

Schools

When they were 15 years old, all noble boys began going to a House of Teaching. This school in Cuzco was taught by Wise Men. Wise Men were people who learned Inca knowledge by heart. They were able to teach their students from memory.

Noble boys learned about the Quechua language, religion, quipus, music, and math.

▲ One of the jobs of a priest was to make offerings at special stones, like this one.

Their learning helped them become government officials or priests.

Both male and female children of the working class did not receive schooling. They learned the skills they needed, such as weaving or farming, from older members of their family.

This is a figure of a local leader in the Incas' decimal administration system.

What Did the Incas Do?

The Incas came up with a new idea for government called **decimal** administration. Decimal is a system of counting based on groups of 10. The Incas' decimal government had many levels. Each person at each level was in charge of 10 other people.

The Incas organized their religion in the same way they ran their government. A high priest was in charge of religious activities. He was in charge of 10 less powerful priests. These priests were in charge of one of the 10 religious areas of the empire. Under these priests were local priests who took care of temples for the different gods.

▲ **The Incas built these terraces to farm crops on.**

Achievements

The Incas knew that it was important to keep close track of different parts of their empire. This is one reason why they built so many roads. They had special runners that stayed in huts built next to the roads. These runners would carry messages from one hut to another, shouting the message to a new runner as soon as they arrived. In this way, it took about two days for Inca government officials to pass news from throughout the empire to the emperor in Cuzco.

The Incas came up with new ideas in farming. They built large **terraces** on mountainsides. Terraces are flat areas on sloped land that look like steps. The Incas built stone walls and then filled them with soil to make terraces. The walls kept the soil from washing away when it rained. The terraces allowed the Incas to farm land that could not be farmed if it was sloped. The Incas dug canals that carried water from springs and rivers to dry parts of the terraces.

The Incas studied the stars and the sky. They used this information to track the movement of the Sun, Moon, and stars. They made a calendar based on these movements. They studied their calendar to decide the best times for planting and religious ceremonies.

End of the Inca Empire

The Inca Empire was the most powerful in South America during the late 1400s and early 1500s. The emperor Huayna Capac, however, died suddenly in 1527. Two of his sons, Huascar and Atahualpa, claimed to be the emperor.

The war between the brothers weakened the Inca Empire. The Inca people were not sure who the emperor should be. Some of the nobles in Cuzco supported Huascar. He took control of the empire first. But many of the Inca people supported Atahualpa who controlled a big part of the army. Atahualpa took over the empire a few years later.

During the late 1400s and early 1500s, explorers from Spain began arriving in the America. The explorers wanted to steal the Inca's gold and silver riches for themselves.

One Spanish explorer was Francisco Pizarro. In 1532, Pizarro and about 170 of his men entered Inca land. Atahualpa left Cuzco to greet the explorers. Pizarro captured

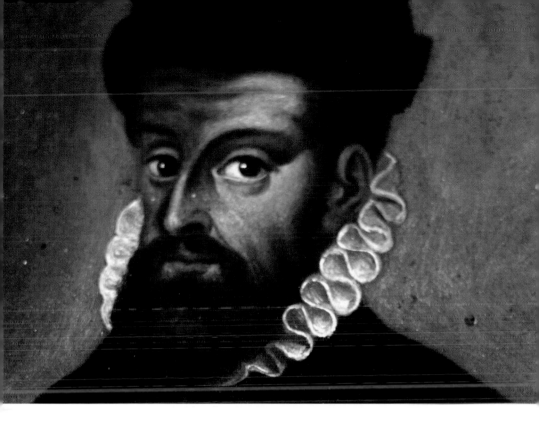

This is a painting of Francisco Pizarro, the Spanish explorer.

Atahualpa and forced the Incas to pay great amounts of gold and silver to get Atahualpa back. Pizarro took the riches, but killed Atahualpa anyway.

Pizarro then went to war with the Incas. In 1535, the Spanish took over Cuzco. The Incas kept fighting, but their empire was over.

Archaeologists study the ruins of Inca buildings to learn about the Incas' way of life.

How Do We Know?

Historians have no written history of the Incas before the 1500s. The Incas used storytelling to pass on their history.

Today, **archaeologists** study Inca ruins to learn about Inca civilization. Archaeologists are scientists who study **ancient** remains. They find out what life was like for the Incas by studying artifacts. An artifact is an object made or used by humans in the past. Inca artifacts include jewelry, metal objects, pottery, and tools.

Many Inca cities and temples still exist today. Their strong walls and buildings make it possible for archaeologists to find out how Inca cities once looked.

Inca Sites

Machu Picchu is one of the most famous Inca sites. This town is northwest of Cuzco high in the Andes. Mountains surround the site on three sides. Machu Picchu was so well hidden that Europeans did not find it until 1911. The town has a palace, a temple for the Sun god, and terraces built for farming.

Another famous Inca site lies on Mount Sara Sara in Peru. The site is about 18,000 feet (6,200 m) above sea level. The Incas performed religious rituals at this site. Archaeologists study remains at the site to learn about the Inca's religious beliefs.

Incas and the Modern World

Today, many Inca ruins still stand in western South America. The city of Cuzco still has many of the walls the Incas built. People travel from around the world to see Cuzco and other Inca ruins.

While many Inca buildings survived, parts of their culture did not. Pizarro and his men

Machu Picchu was an Inca city built high on a mountaintop.

killed many of Incas living in Cuzco. The explorers forced the Incas to accept Spanish beliefs. But some Inca ideas in clothing, farming, fishing, music, and making pottery still survive today.

Some descendants of the Incas are practicing their culture. Millions of people speak Quechua as their only language. They make cloth and pottery as the ancient Incas did.

Glossary

ally (AL-eye)—two or more groups that work together toward a common goal

ancestor (AN-sess-tur)—a member of someone's family who lived a long time ago

ancient (AYN-shunt)—very old

archaeologist (ar-kee-OL-uh-jist)—a scientist who studies ancient remains

architect (AR-ki-tekt)—a person who designs buildings and oversees their construction

capture (KAP-chur)—to take over by force

culture (KUHL-chur)—the traditions and ways of a group

custom (KUHSS-tom)—something that you do regularly

decimal (DESS-uh-muhl)—units of 10

empire (EM-pire)—a group of countries with one ruler

ethnic (ETH-nik)—to do with a group of people sharing the same national origins, language, or culture

fortress (FOR-triss)—a place that is strengthened against attack

generation (jen-uh-RAY-shuhn)—a group of people born around the same time

local (LOH-kuhl)—something that is close to or from the neighborhood where you live

official (uh-FISH-uhl)—someone who works for the government

organized (OR-guh-nized)—something that is planned and run well

pottery (POT-ur-ee)—objects made of clay, such as pots, bowls, vases, and cups

quipu (KEE-poo)—an Inca counting device made up of strings and knots

social (SOH-shuhl)—having to do with the way that people live together as a society

subject (SUHB-jikt)—a person who lives in an empire or kingdom

terrace (TER-iss)—a flat area on sloped land

tropical (TROP-uh-kuhl)—hot and rainy

Internet Sites

Ancient Latin America
http://emuseum.mankato.msus.edu/prehistory
/latinamerica/

Empire of the Incas
http://www.sscf.ucsb.edu/~ogburn/inca/

Inca
http://www.kent.wednet.edu/KSD/SB/Ancient/
Inca.html

Inca—Britannica.com
http://www.britannica.com/bcom/eb/article/0/
0,5716,43190+1+42237,00.html

The Inca Project
http://www.best.com/~swanson/inca/eg_inca_
intro.html

NOVA Online—Ice Mummies of the Inca
http://www.pbs.org/wgbh/nova/peru/

Department of Anthropology, University of California at Santa Barbara
Department of Anthropology
University of California
Santa Barbara, CA 93106

Museum of Archaeology and Ethnology
Department of Archaeology
Simon Fraser University
8888 University Drive
Burnaby, BC V5A 1S6
Canada

Index